T.L. OSBORN

GW00706145

HEALTH
RENEWED

BOOKS BY THE OSBORNS

BELIEVERS IN ACTION – Apostolic – Rejuvenating

THE BEST OF LIFE – Seven Energizing Dynamics

BIBLICAL HEALING – Seven Miracle Keys
4 Visions – 50+ yrs. of Proof – 324 Merged Bible Vs.

FIVE CHOICES FOR WOMEN WHO WIN –
21st Century Options

GOD'S BIG PICTURE – An Impelling Gospel Classic

GOD'S LOVE PLAN – The Awesome Discovery

THE GOOD LIFE – A Mini-Bible School – 1,467 Ref.

THE GOSPEL ACCORDING TO T.L. & DAISY –
Their Life & World Ministry – 510 pg. Pictorial

HEALING THE SICK – A Living Classic

HOW TO BE BORN AGAIN – The Miracle Book

IF I WERE A WOMAN –
T.L. Encourages Gender Equality under Redemption

JESUS AND WOMEN – Big Questions Answered

LIFE – TRIUMPH OVER TRAGEDY –
A True Story of Life After Death

THE MESSAGE THAT WORKS –
T.L.'s Revealing Manifesto on Biblical Faith

NEW LIFE FOR WOMEN – Reality Re-focused

THE POWER OF POSITIVE DESIRE –
An Invigorating Faith Perspective

SOULWINNING – OUTSIDE THE SANCTUARY –
A Classic on Biblical Christianity & Human Dignity

WOMEN & SELF-ESTEEM – Divine Royalty Unrestrai~

THE WOMAN BELIEVER – Awareness of God's Desi~

WOMAN WITHOUT LIMITS –
Unmuzzled – Unfettered – Unimpeded

YOU ARE GOD'S BEST – Transforming Life Discover~

OSBORN
PUBLISHERS

P.O. Box 10, Tulsa, OK 74102 USA
Tel: 918/743-6231
Fax: 918/749-0339   E-mail: OSFO@aol.com
www.OSBORN.ORG

Canada: Box 281, Adelaide St. Post Sta., Toronto M5C 2J4
England: Box 148, Birmingham B3 2LG
(A Registered Charity)

BIBLE QUOTATIONS in this book are from the King James Authorized Version (1611) unless otherwise noted. Other languages and versions have been considered. Scriptures may be personalized, paraphrased, abridged or conformed to the *person* and *tense* of their contextual application, to foster clarity and individual acceptance. Chapter and verse references enable the reader to verify accuracy.

The Author

ISBN 0-87943-119-9
Copyright 2002 by T.L. Osborn
Printed in the United States of America
All Rights Reserved

CONTENTS

Chapter 1:
No Longer Victimized 7

Chapter 2:
The Destructive Decline 11

Chapter 3:
The Healer 15

Chapter 4:
Sickness was Never God's Plan 18

Chapter 5:
Your Debt is Abolished 23

Chapter 6:
Your Health is Paid For 26

Chapter 7:
Christ's Life is Your Life 43

Chapter 8:
The Prayer-Confession 46

Chapter 9:
Osborn Ministry Review 51

Dedicated to

all who desire

to live in renewed

health, emotionally,

spiritually, mentally

and physically

Chapter One

NO LONGER VICTIMIZED

ONE OF THE MOST urgent human needs is for physical health. In human society, minds are distorted, disease and suffering are rampant, despondency and disillusionment reigns, hospitals are over-run. Psychiatrists and psychologists are often as bewildered as their patients are.

A great majority of people psychologically transmit their spiritual and mental problems to their physical bodies so that, in spite of the achievements of medical science, they become incurable from a human point of view.

The Source Of Sickness

You may be in need of physical health, facing the possibility of an incurable illness. Many people think it is normal to live subject to disease and suffering. They never question the source of this menacing dilemma. If a symptom appears, they rush to their doctor, then to their pharmacist with foreboding apprehension.

Many assume that God may be using sickness for some mysterious purpose in their lives. Or they may think that it can teach them some lesson in patience, humility, endurance or submission.

God provides physical health for you so that you can be at your best for *Him*, for *others* and for *yourself*. You need good health to be able to realize accomplishments, to fulfill your duties and desires in life among your family, in your neighborhood, in your business and in your world.

Is It God—Or Fate?

There is a power greater than disease. God has bestowed His healing love upon all who embrace Him as Savior. Be receptive to the Great Physician who will come to you as He has to multitudes worldwide.

The truths of healing expressed in this section can be as alive as God is because *His Words are Spirit and they are Life.*[Joh.6:63]

As we have proclaimed the truths of God's healing love worldwide, tens of thousands of sick and suffering people have been miraculously healed while listening. Jesus said, *the truth will make you free.*[Joh.8:32]

We did not know about their cases any more than we know about yours. We did not lay our hands on them and pray for them individually any more than I can lay my hands on you and pray for you now. They simply heard and believed, and God made His Word good in their lives. That can happen to you as you continue reading these pages.

Chapter Two

THE DESTRUCTIVE DECLINE

GOD CREATED Adam and Eve perfect, physically, mentally, spiritually, and He placed them in the Garden of Eden amidst His abundance. They were not sick or incapacitated by disease.

God's plan for those whom He created *in His own image* ^{Gen.1:26-27; 5:1-2} could never have included disease and infirmity. If He had designed them for pain and malady, would He have created them in such perfection?

God's message is about showing you *The Way* back to the paradise enjoyed before Adam and Eve sinned. His plan for humanity has never changed. He wills His best for all who believe.

Did God Mean What He Said?

Satan, the tempter, persuaded Adam and Eve to doubt God's Word. The cunning question that he posed to them was: *Has God said?*[Gen.3:1]

They concluded that God did not mean what He said when He warned: *Of the tree of the knowledge of good and evil, you shall **not** eat of it: for in the day that you eat it you shall surely die.*[Gen.2:17] They disobeyed the Lord, and were consequently banished from the paradise that He had created for them, and they began to die.

From that day, Adam and Eve became subjugated by Satan and their descendants exhibited the sad results of doubting God's Word. All that was perfect in them began to deteriorate. That process continues today. With every sin committed, something dies in the one who sins.

Subversion Of Faith

Happiness degenerates into sadness; love, into hatred. Life is plagued by disease and eventual death. Beauty turns to ashes. Faith is subverted by distrust, and confidence is displaced by deception. Healthy bodies become subject to the destructive power and influence of Satan who *came to steal and kill and destroy.*[Joh.10:10]

God Has Not Abandoned Us

The twin evils, sin and sickness, have

marched hand-in-hand throughout all generations since Adam and Eve. The human mind and heart have degenerated through sin and corruption.

In spite of the prodigious achievements of modern science, incurable diseases still threaten human society.

Is there an answer? Has God abandoned us to this plight? Is physical healing part of His redemptive plan for humanity?

Chapter Three

THE HEALER

GOD ANNOUNCES, *I am the Lord who heals you.* ^{Exo.15:26} or, *I am the Lord your physician.*

You may find it difficult to reconcile this with so much sickness in our world, with so many innocent people suffering, and with so much negative religious teaching about disease.

If you are cognizant of God's redemptive plan for humanity, you will know that His will is for you to have physical health as well as spiritual salvation and material blessings.

John wrote, *I wish above all things that you may prosper (be helped, to succeed in affairs)* *and be in **health**, even as your soul prospers.* 3Jo.2

When Jesus Christ died on the Cross, the Bible says that He bore our physical diseases in the same way that He bore our sins and our iniquities. So the question is not: Did He bear our physical diseases? The question is: Why?

The same verb in both Hebrew and Greek that is used to state that Jesus Christ bore our spiritual iniquities is also used to state that He bore our physical diseases. Isa.53:4-5; Mat.8:16-17; 1Pe.2:24

Christ's Vicarious Intervention

Why did Christ bear them? The answer constitutes the essence of Good News to those who are physically ill. He did it so that you do not have to do it. He did it as your personal substitute. That is why you can be healed.

He bore your diseases so that *the Life also of Jesus might be made manifest in your mortal flesh, or bodies.* ^{2Co.4:10}

That is *The MESSAGE That WORKS.*

Chapter Four

SICKNESS WAS NEVER GOD'S PLAN

IT WAS NEVER God's plan for His people to be sick and weak or to suffer pain and disease.

The plague of physical disease came about after Adam and Eve bowed to Satan's temptation. *Sin was conceived. And when it was finished, it brought forth death.*[Jam.1:15]

This beautiful couple whom God created *in His own image and likeness* [Gen.1:26-27: 5:1-2] had to be banished from His presence because He cannot co-exist or cohabit with sin. The seeds of sin produced their harvest and humanity began to deteriorate and die.

The wickedness of people was great in the earth, and every imagination of the thoughts of their hearts were only evil continually. Gen.6:5-6
The lifestyle of people deteriorated into a veritable breeding ground for disease and decay. Disharmony and deceit, jealousy and hatred, envy and lust, violence and murder poisoned every fiber of the human spirit and that poison invaded the physical body too.

God Planned *"Redemption"*

Deuteronomy, Chapter 28, outlines the destructive harvest of disobedience to God. It enumerates a forbidding litany of physical diseases which humankind suffers: *Pestilence, vexation, comsumption, fever, inflammation, extreme burning, mildew, the botch of Egypt, emerods, scab, itch, madness, blindness, astonishment of heart, oppression, violence, smiting in the knees and in the legs, sore botch, hunger, thirst, nakedness, want of all things, distress, plagues, sicknesses [and so much more].* [Due.28:15,20-22,27-29,35,60-61,65-67]

Then a comprehensive footnote is added to the gruesome catalog: *Also every sickness and every plague which is not written in the book of this law.* [v.61]

But God, who is Love and Life—God who created man and woman *in His own image* [Gen.1:26-47; 5:1-2]—could not abandon His dream.

As Adam and Eve left His presence to be subjugated by Satan's scourge of depravity and despair, God was conceiving His plan of redemption to bring them back into His presence. He made *The Way* to rescue and legally deliver you and me from Satan who had defrauded us.

God's Law decrees that those who sin will reap the harvest of their sins. *The soul that sins, it shall die.*[Eze.18:4,20] *The wages of sin is death.*[Rom.6:23]

But ***all*** have sinned.[Rom.3:23; 5:12] *Wherefore, as by one person [Adam] sin entered into the world, and death by sin; so death passed upon all, for all have sinned.*[Rom.5:12] So the harvest of sin was inescapable. All would suffer, degenerate and die.

Only an innocent, sinless One could take our place and assume our judgment on our behalf. If someone without sin would assume and endure all of the punishment that our sins deserved, then we could be exonerated and declared no longer guilty. But since *all* had sinned, no substitute could be found.[Isa.59:16; 63:5]

Then God's Love-idea prevailed. He gave

His Son as *a ransom* for us.[1Ti.2:5-6; Mar.10:45]
Jesus Christ, the innocent One, suffered the
penalty that we deserved, so that we could be
acquitted and He could declare us *not
guilty.*[Rom.5:9 LB]

That is the message that we declare around
the world. It is *The MESSAGE That WORKS.*

Chapter Five

YOUR DEBT IS ABOLISHED

THE GOSPEL IS *Good News*. What Good News? It is the Good News of what Jesus did for us on the Cross. He bore the punishment of our sins so that we do not need to be punished. By expunging our record, He delivered us from the consequences of our sins, which included disease.

The great redemptive chapter of Isaiah 53 says, *Certainly He has borne our sicknesses and carried our pains.*[v.4] When Jesus suffered our penalty on the Cross, *He was being wounded for our transgressions, bruised for our iniquities: the chastisement of our peace was upon Him; and with His stripes we are healed.* Isa.53:5

If Jesus suffered our diseases and bore our pains, then logically *we **are** healed.*

This is like saying: "Your friend paid your debt, and by his payment, your debt no longer exists. So you are free." Your debt is wiped from the record, once it has been paid. You have no more debt. You cannot pay the same debt twice. Once paid, your debt is expunged.

The *Message* Confirmed

That is God's message of Good News. Jesus said, "When you *know that truth, it makes you free.*" Joh.8:32 In other words, when that Good News is announced or taught or preached or written or recorded, then heard, it (the Gospel) *is the power of God unto salvation.* Rom.1:16

It (the Gospel) is the message that Christ *confirms.*[Mar.16:20] He will confirm this truth today, in your life, as you read with faith and reverence.

Jesus announced: *For the Lord has consecrated me and sent me with Good News for people, to heal the brokenhearted, to tell the prisoners **they are free**, to tell captives **they are released**.*[Isa.61:1 (Moffatt)]

Announcing these facts puts God's miraculous power to work among the listeners. This is what we have experienced worldwide. We proclaim these facts. People hear them and believe them, and God manifests them in their lives.

Chapter Six

YOUR HEALTH IS PAID FOR

THIS MESSAGE OF Good News is, as we stated above, *the power of God for the salvation of everyone who believes it.*Rom.1:16

I cannot explain how Jesus suffered our diseases, bore our pains, and endured the judgment of our sins on the Cross so many years ago, but I believe it. It is not logical. That is why *the preaching of the Cross is to them that perish foolishness: but to us who are saved it is the power of God.*1Co.1:18

When we believe in our hearts and confess with our mouths what the Bible says that Jesus did for us in His vicarious death,Rom.10:9-10 then

God confirms it by His miracle power. Jesus said, *Only believe.*Mar.5:36

Christ paid for our complete healing when He died. He is the Lord *who heals all our diseases.* Psa.103:3 He paid for our healing when *He carried our diseases and suffered our pains, taking the stripes by which we were healed.*Isa.53:4-5 (Literal)

It is finished now.Joh.19:30 Our health is paid for. Our diseases were laid upon Christ.Mat.8:17 He took them away forever. Healing belongs to us now. It is God's gift. This is why the Lord reveals Himself as *the Lord who heals us... the Lord our physician.* Exo.15:26

Satan has no right to lay on us what God laid on Jesus Christ at the Cross.

Redemptive Facts For Faith

The Lord has laid on Him the iniquity of us all. [Isa.53:6]

For the transgression of people He was stricken. [v.8]

It pleased the Lord to bruise Him...and make His soul an offering for sin. [v.10]

For He shall bear their iniquity. [v.11]

He bore the sins of many. [v.12]

He was wounded for our transgressions. He was bruised for our iniquities: the chastisement of our peace was upon Him. [v5]

Certainly He has borne our sicknesses and carried our pains. [v.4 (Literal)] *With His stripes we are healed.* [v.5]

Himself took our infirmities, and bare our

sicknesses. ^{Mat.8:17} Why? So that we do not have to—so that we can be healed and enjoy health and strength to serve Him by serving people.

He Himself bore our sins in His own body on the tree. Why? *So that we, being dead to sins, should live unto righteousness.* What is the result? *By His stripes we were healed* ^{1Pe.2:24} —spiritually, mentally, physically.

Deadly Toxins
Life-Giving Gifts

When sin entered the human family, its consequences included physical sickness, malady, suffering and death.

The devastation of deceit and evil, the decadence of lust and envy, the noxious gangrene of hatred and vengeance, the morbid corruption of sin and rebellion all impose their destructive toll on the human body as toxic fall-out.

Salvation and healing are free gifts from God to rescue and to heal human persons, not only from the evil of sin in their hearts and spirits, but from the terrifying physical effects evidenced in the nerves, organs, tissues and glands of their bodies.

This Great Salvation

*Jesus Christ Himself bore **our** sins,* [1Pe.2:24] so that we may be saved and forgiven. *He took **our** infirmities, and bore **our** sicknesses,* [Mat.8:17] so that we may be healed and made whole.

Forgiveness of sins and physical healing are both part of salvation. Spiritual and physical healing, according to God's Word, are to be received together. Salvation includes physical as well as spiritual health. Jesus always healed both.

Total Healing

Who forgives all your iniquities; who heals all your diseases. Psa.103:3

Which is it easier to say, Your sins are forgiven you; or to say, Arise, and walk? Mat.9:5

For this people's heart is waxed gross, and their ears dull of hearing, and their eyes they have closed: lest at any time they should see with their eyes, and hear with their ears, and should understand with their heart, and should be **converted***, and I should* **heal** *them.* Mat.13:15

Is any sick among you?... The prayer of faith shall **save** *the sick, and the Lord shall*

*raise them up; and if they have committed sins,
they shall be **forgiven**.* ^{Jam.5:14-15}

The Great Physician offers total health—
spiritually, mentally and physically.

T.L. and Bishop LaDonna Osborn minister across ten major cities of the ex-Soviet Union, proclaiming the miracle-producing gospel to packed auditoriums in every city, and giving a full set of Osborns' 10 books to each adult.

T.L. Osborn ministers the miracle Gospel in Moscow, Russia.

After Daisy's death, the Osborn daughter, Dr. LaDonna ministered with her father in their trans-evangelical seminar and public miracle crusade in Medellin, Colombia.

T.L. Osborn

T.L. Osborn ministers under Eckman's 10,000 seat tent, Sweden.

Only miracles can convince the ex-Soviet nations about Christ.

Tons of Osborn books are given to believers in the Antioquia Province of S. America.

LaDonna Osborn

Swedes; famous for Missions, respond to T.L.'s dynamic preaching.

"We're bringing hope and faith to tens of thousands who have known nothing but Godless communism."

Osborn brings miracle life to thousands of Ukrainians.

Dr. LaDonna in Beijing, dedicates tons of T.L.'s book, *"Healing the Sick"*, in Mandarin Chinese language.

e fifth of the world lives hina. *"Why should one hear the gospel e before everyone heard it once?"* We eeding China NOW.

医治
疾病

Osborn books in Mandarin, seeding for China's great soul harvest.

China has influenced the world or over 5,000 years. Now, the old is giving way to the *new*. God's LOVE and redemptive lan for humanity is the only ope for these millions.

T.L. & LaDonna Osborn Miracle Crusade–Medellin, Colombia

LaDonna Osborn

T.L. & LaDonna Osborn Miracle-Life Conferenc
Amlaty, Kyrghyzstan, an ex-Soviet Republic. The
Osborn books in Russian are given to every adul

T.L. & Daisy Osborn Mass Miracle Crusade – Bogota, S. America

...usands attend the T.L. & LaDonna Osborn ...cle Life Conference in this ancient Moslem ...on of Kyrghyzstan–bordering West China.

T.L. Osborn

Dr. LaDonna Osborn has been involved with her parents in miracle evagelism from her youth. The same anointing that has rested upon T.L. ar Daisy, is evident in LaDonna's own global ministry. As the gospel is pro claimed by either T.L. or LaDonna, crutches, canes, braces and wheel-chairs are hoisted to signal miracles received through the power of God word. As in Jesus' day, *The power of the Lord was present to heal.* [Lu. 5:]

LaDonna & T.L. strategize global crusades and literature-distribution. Their preaching is always confirmed by miracles. TONS of their books seed church leaders and believers for spiritual harvests, impacting nations with Christ's gospel.

"What Christ's power and love have done for others, it will do in your life. This book contains keys of biblical healing for YOU." — LaDonna & T.L.

Signs, wonders and miracles confirm the ministry of Dr. LaDonna as she promulgates the healing gospel in her global crusades.

Following T.L.'s message and mass prayer for healing, this young man marches across the platform (inset) with steel brace and shoes lifted high, to show the miracle God has done for him.

Chapter Seven

CHRIST'S LIFE IS YOUR LIFE

SINCE JESUS CHRIST bore the sins and diseases of the whole world, He now wants to enter people's lives and become their Savior and their Healer—their Lord.

He said that when we love Him, *the Father will love us, and they would come to us, and make their abode with us.*Joh.14:23

He says, *I am come that you may have life, and that you may have it more abundantly.*Joh.10:10 This new life is for whoever believes.

When you accept Jesus, His abundant and miraculous Life becomes yours. It is not His will that you suffer either sin or disease.

Paul said that *the Life of Jesus might be made manifest (not only in your spirit, but) also in your* **mortal flesh**.^{2Co.4:11} Christ's life becomes your life. His righteousness becomes yours. He and the Father *make their abode with you.*^{Joh.14:23} *You are built for an* **habitation** *of God,*^{Eph.2:22} *whose* **house** *you are* ^{Heb.3:6} because *Christ* **dwells** *in your heart by faith.* ^{Eph.3:17} *You are the temple of God, and the Spirit of God* **dwells** *in you.*^{1Co.3:16} *Your* **body** *is the* **temple** *of the Holy Ghost.*^{1Co.6:19} *Jesus Christ is* **in** *you.*^{2Co.13:5; Col.1:27} Paul added: *Christ lives* **in** *the believer.*^{Gal.2:20}

The Lord says: *Behold, I stand at the door, and knock: if any one hear my voice, and open the door, I will come in and will sup with them and they with me.* ^{Rev.3:20}

Paradise Of Blessings

When humanity's sins were punished and the account of our rebellion was wiped out, anyone who would embrace Christ could then be reconciled to God and restored to the paradise of blessing which He created for people.

Jesus came to the level of our needs and became accountable for our sins. He suffered the punishment we deserved. His blood was shed for us. It washed our record clean. [Rev.1:5; Eph.1:7]

As soon as any person understands this, the Lord is ready to enter their life. He wants to be their Lord and Savior, [Sect.I] their Peace, [Sect.II] their Shepherd, [Sect.III]—and their P*hysician*. [Sect.IV] He wills that His Life be manifested in you and in me, physically as well as spiritually.

The Bible says, *With long life will I satisfy them and show them my salvation.* [Psa.91:10,16 NRSV] OUR HEALTH IS RENEWED.

Chapter Eight

THE PRAYER-CONFESSION

NOW THAT YOU REALIZE where sickness came from and that it was never the design of your Heavenly Father that His children suffer physically, make this confession to Him in humility and in faith.

He invites you: *Call unto me, and I will answer you.*^{Jer.33:3} *Ask, and you shall receive, that your joy may be full.*^{Joh.16:23-24} *For everyone who asks receives.*^{Mat.7:8} Say this to Him aloud:

DEAR LORD: I thank you for announcing that *you are the Lord, my physician.*^{Exo.15:26} I am grateful to know that your plan for me includes

physical healing.

Before I knew that sickness, suffering and pain resulted from that first rebellion by Adam and Eve, I presumed that there was no escape from physical disease in my life.

Now I know that sickness is part of the result of Adam and Eve being banished from your presence. They were subjugated by Satan whose purpose is *to kill, to steal and to destroy them,* [Joh.10:10] and disease is part of the consequence of banishment from your divine presence.

You did not abandon us in slavery to the Evil One. After Adam and Eve disobeyed your Word, we all deserved to die. But you sent your Son to be *the propitiation for the sins of the whole world.* Rom.3:24-25

I NOW UNDERSTAND that Jesus suffered not only the punishment of my sins, but also the consequences of my fallen nature, part of which is disease and pain.

Now I know that Jesus Christ *of a certainty took upon Himself all of my diseases and suffered all of my pains* Isa.53:4-5 (Literal) **so that I can be completely** *healed*.

Lord, your body was beaten beyond recognition. *Your visage was marred more than any other man.* Isa.52:14 **Your back was striped. When they beat you,** *they plowed your back: they made long their furrows.* Psa.129:3 **You were**

bruised and torn.[Isa.53:5] Now I know that my sicknesses were laid on you.[Mat.8:17] You suffered them for me so that I could be healed.

I THANK YOU LORD, for sending me this message of *Good News*. I receive your miracle life in me, here and now. *By your stripes I have been healed*.[Isa.53:5; 1Pe.2:24]

The grace and life of Jesus Christ which now abides in me, heals me of both sin and disease. I am saved and healed—and free.

Satan has lost his dominion over me. No sin can subjugate or condemn me. No sickness has the right to destroy my body which is now *the temple of the Holy Spirit*.[1Co.6:19]

JESUS, YOU ARE MY LORD. From today, I appropriate the blessing of physical healing because you are my Life. You are with me and in me now!^Joh.14:17 My *HEALTH IS RENEWED.* Amen!

Chapter Nine

OSBORN MINISTRY REVIEW

THE GLOBAL MISSION of Christianity is *to witness of Christ and of His resurrection to all the world, to every creature.*[Mar.16:15] The Apostle Paul was consumed with this passion.

He said, *Whoever shall call on the name of the Lord shall be saved* [Rom.10:13] if they *believe in their heart that God raised Jesus from the dead, and if they confess Him as their Lord.*[Rom.10:9-10]

Then Paul asked the pivotal questions that characterize this ***Global Mission of Christianity***.

How shall they call on him in whom they have not believed? and how shall they believe in him of whom they have not heard? and how shall they hear without a preacher? And how shall they preach except they be sent? Rom.10:14-15

A Family Quest for Souls

T.L. and Daisy Osborn shared a worldwide ministry for over five decades. Their lives together exemplified *The **Global Mission** of Christianity,* demonstrating for over a half-century the passion and commitment that motivated Paul in his unrelenting quest to bring the light of the gospel to those living in darkness. 2Co.4:6; Acs.26:18

Dr. Daisy's earthly ministry ended with her demise at 2:53 a.m. on the morning of May 27, 1995, but the outreaches of the Osborns' world ministry continue under the leadership of T.L.

and the Osborn daughter, Dr. LaDonna, who now shares the preaching, the ministry to the sick, and the teaching in their continuing global crusades and Miracle-Life seminars abroad.

As CEO and Vice-President of *OSBORN International,* LaDonna's expertise is making possible the expansion of the Osborn ministry into many **new fields** such as the vast nation of *Russia,* nations of *French-speaking Africa* and of *Eurasia* (republics of the ex-soviet union) and the world's largest nation, *China,* and through the world wide web, www.osborn.org.

This *review* of the Osborns' global ministry that has reached millions for Christ in more than eighty nations, is included in this book to inspire young men and women to bear the *Gospel Torch* and to carry Christ's message, *into all the world.*^{Mar.16:15}

The Global Saga Continues

During more than a half-century, T.L. and Daisy proclaimed the Gospel together to millions of people in seventy-three nations. The biblical programs and concepts for evangelism that they have engendered continue to make an unprecedented impact in our world.

Although T.L. is now is his advancing years, the Osborn world ministry continues unabated in this 21st Century. Following Daisy's demise, T.L. has persevered in his global evangelism crusades, and his daughter, Dr. LaDonna, has expanded her ministries of soulwinning, of preaching and teaching, and of Church leadership to every continent.

Today, the anointed ministry of the Osborns' daughter, Dr. LaDonna, is a leading force in their global outreaches. Her preaching, teaching and miracle ministries are promulgating gospel evangelism among the nations and are influencing international church leadership both at home and abroad.

Osborn daughter, Dr. LaDonna, now carries the *Torch of the Gospel* into this century's new frontiers, focusing on gospel-neglected areas of the world such as China, Russia, French-speaking Africa and the ex-communist nations of Eurasia.

The Dual Mission

In 1987, the Lord visited LaDonna, calling her to pastoral ministry. On January 9, 1989, she became the official pastor of Tulsa's *Int'l Gospel Center*. As she has led the church, her focus has been on winning the lost, then on building each convert into effective witnesses for Christ. That dual mission has shaped her life and ministry in a way that combines her world evangelism ministry with her international church leadership.

In addition to being Vice President and CEO of *OSBORN International*—the world missionary institution founded by T.L. and Daisy Osborn in 1949, LaDonna is founder and bishop of the *International Gospel Center Fellowship of Churches and Ministries (IGCFCM),* a network of over 200 pastors and churches, with headquarters at Tulsa, Oklahoma.

She is a member of the *College of Bishops* for the *International Communion of Charismatic Churches (ICCC),* representing over 7,000 pastors, 9,000 churches and more than *ten million* believers, spanning every continent.

LaDonna personifies the dual image that Christ gave to His Church; 1) To bring people to HIM, then 2) To build *HIM* into people. She says, "The passion of Jesus drove Him to the *cross*. Now His passion drives us to the *lost*."

Passion For Souls

As a world evangelist, Dr. LaDonna's passion to help people discover their purpose in Christ *impels her to the remote corners of the earth* where she preaches and teaches with clarity, boldness, and miracle confirmation.

As a pastor, her passion to build people into dedicated representatives for Christ *motivates her in a life-changing ministry of teaching the truths of Redemption*—truths that lift believers to their full potential in Christ.

As a bishop of more than 200 pastors and churches within her own network—plus her activities in the ICCC and other organizations, her passion is to help Christian leaders grasp

God's vision for their world. *This drives her in apostolic leadership that is seeding new life and biblical action in churches both at home and abroad.*

LaDonna's unique style and broad world-view are sought after as significant gifts to the Body of Christ, challenging the Church to *BE CHRIST'S BODY IN ACTION—Out Where The People Are.*

Her classic teaching on *Redemption* is widely acclaimed as the most practical and significant material for grounding new believers and for training Church leaders in the *Dynamics of Christ-Centered Ministry.*

Wherever she ministers, physical healing miracles distinguish her ministry and demonstrate Christ's living presence with her.

Her presentation of the all encompassing

Bible message of the gospel has become the *hallmark of her ministry* among the masses and within the Church both at home and abroad.

Like the Apostle Paul, LaDonna says, *I am not ashamed of the gospel of Christ, for it is the power of God to salvation to everyone who believes.* [Rom.1:16]

Model for Balance

Bishop LaDonna's role in *21st Century Church Leadership* is a modern day continuation of apostolic ministry. She models the essential balance of *gospel evangelism* and of *Church discipline.*

She is a prophetic voice reminding the Church and its leaders that *its mission is to share the message of Christ with all people of the world.* She believes that every soul won to

Christ must be drawn into the local church where they can grow in God's grace and be trained for Christ-centered ministry.

Dr. LaDonna's maxim for ministry is: 1) *Establish people in Christ,* then 2) *Establish Christ in people.* She insists that every believer is *CHRIST'S LIFE AND LOVE—IN FLESH.*

She believes: *The World is the **Heart** of the Church.* And: *The Church is the **Hope** of the World.* She contends that without the *World, the Church is **meaningless** and without the Church, the World is **hopeless**.*

Her passion is to impart this vital knowledge to pastors and leaders every-where, helping them...

1)   *to grasp God's perspective of our hurting world and*

2)   *to discover how to convince non-*

Christians that Jesus Christ is alive and that the Bible is true in this 21st Century.

Colonialism—Nationalism—Evangelism

Dr. LaDonna Osborn knows the ministry of World Evangelism. She has lived on the front lines of global soulwinning from the days of *colonialism,* through the turbulent years of *nationalism,* and into this century of *evangelism and national Church growth* when the largest churches on earth are being raised up by national pastors in what was previously referred to as *"3rd World Mission Fields."*

Her spiritual insight and biblical knowledge combines to make her *redemptive teaching* not only apostolic and biblical but dynamic in its influence on pastors, leaders and gospel workers.

When dates can be synchronized, LaDonna ministers with her father, T.L. Osborn, in Mass

Miracle Crusades and in Miracle Life Seminars. She shares the crusade preaching, the public mass ministry to the sick, and the Seminar teaching, bringing new faith, hope, love and LIFE to thousands of church leaders, pastors, Bible School students and gospel workers.

The Christian Mission

The Osborn ministry with its international influence and its arsenal of soulwinning tools and programs, is committed to apostolic ministry that will help the gospel ministers and the peoples of this Century to know...

1) That the Bible is as valid today as it ever was,

2) That the mission of every believer is to win the lost to Christ,

3) That every soul won can become Christ's representative, and

4) That miracles, signs and wonders will continue to be what distinguish Christianity from being just another religion.